Summary

of

Us vs. Them
Ian Bremmer

Conversation Starters

By Paul Adams
Book Habits

MW00897035

Please Note: This is an unofficial Conversation Starters guide. If you have not yet read the original work, you can purchase the original book here.

We hope you enjoy this complimentary guide from BookHabits. Our mission is to aid readers and reading groups with quality thought-provoking material to in the discovery and discussions on some of today's favorite books.

Tips for Using Conversation Starters:

EVERY GOOD BOOK CONTAINS A WORLD FAR DEEPER THAN the surface of its pages. Questions herein are designed to bring us beneath the surface of the page and invite us into the world that lives on. These questions can be used to:

- Foster a deeper understanding of the book
- Promote an atmosphere of discussion for groups
- Assist in the study of the book, either individually or corporately
- Explore unseen realms of the book as never seen before

Table of Contents

Introducing *Us vs. Them*

*U*s vs. Them: The Failure of Globalism is a book by Ian Bremmer. The book provides a survey of current geopolitical developments around the world, featuring areas where unrest is most apparent. The author thinks that there is global turmoil and globalization is largely to blame for this. Recent developments show that nations are becoming more closed and people becoming tribal. The grand project of creating an international order does not anymore appear to be possible. Bremmer believes globalization has done good things. It has enabled economic growth and helped many populations out of poverty. This, however, has also led to economic insecurity for many more, causing fissures on existing cohesive societies. The result is what critics call "an era of backlash politics." The book cites that political conflict is not anymore about the divide between the left and the right or between the West and the non-West. It is between the rich and those whose economic status is unstable and seek protection from threatening economic competition, foreigners, and technological change. The author shows how globalization has destabilized the United States, Europe, and the developing world particularly countries like Mexico, Turkey, and Brazil. He says nations have to make stark choices; they could start building walls or they could create new arrangements that bind citizens and governments together that allow both parties to better deal with a world of increasing interdependence. Bremmer cites the initial promise of globalization, that of free trade lifting the poor out of poverty while antagonisms between left and right would dissolve allowing liberal values to triumph. He says this is now a fantasy as events in the past few years have shown. The world is seeing the rise of nationalist and populist politicians who lead their countries in attacking the media, other political leaders, and the corporate elite in their efforts to blame "them" for the economic uncertainty that populations are going through. The author gives five factors that are behind the divisions between "us" and "them." The first is Economics, which shows that the gap between the elite and the poor has widened over the years. "Forty-two people in the world have the same wealth as the bottom 50 percent," he writes. He explains that "when infrastructure spending, public school systems, health care and the like are tied directly to the economic fortunes of a community, it compounds problems of inequality." The second factor is Society and Culture. Workers are threatened by other people flowing across borders because they see this as threats to their livelihoods, lives, entitlements, and status. "Donald Trump understood this better than any of his political rivals in the U.S." and his supporters continue to believe him "because no one else in the United States can credibly promise to defend their interests against establishment disdain." The other factors are Security, Technology and the internet, and Technology and automation. In the book's introduction, Bremmer shares his family's working-class origins, his rise to professional and academic success, and the fulfillment of his American dream. He asks himself why the American dream cannot work for everybody else. In Chapter One, he starts with a quote from William Ernest Henley: "I am the master of my fate, I am the captain of my soul."

Kirkus Reviews says the book is a clear and logical analysis of the phenomena of Trump and Brexit. A "lucid and provocative" book, it gives a warning of what could happen in the future. *Publishers Weekly* cites the author's analysis of developments in countries like Nigeria, Venezuela, Saudi Arabia, India, China, and Russia and shows the common factors that incite the "us vs. them" mentality: lack of employment opportunities, large youth populations, and charismatic politicians who promote divisive ideas. He predicts that these countries "will erect physical and technological 'walls' to keep people in line, and Europe and the United States will follow suit, becoming more protectionist as the developing world struggles." The book closes with a chapter on the relevance of a social contract that binds governments and their citizens. Bremmer says that the mentality of "us vs. them" will intensify "before governments change their ways." The review thinks Bremmer gives "an astute but not optimistic analysis" which could be "difficult reading for those overwhelmed by the current political climate." A review by the *Wall Street Journal* says Bremmer's view is dark and pessimistic that he "even frets about places where recent social and economic progress has been great — China, India, and Turkey...even Russia." It quotes Bremmer: "It's one thing for government to transfer large amounts of wealth to people who need it...it's another to provide them with the services that middle-class citizens expect." He thinks some countries will struggle with providing services for its citizens, particularly those with rapidly aging populations like Japan, Germany, and the Nordic countries. The review cites Bremmer's analysis of the global use of robotics and artificial intelligence technology. This will accordingly reduce "the low-wage advantage that helps poor countries...A shoe manufacturer in Kentucky is better off replacing a middle-wage worker with a no-wage robot than with a low-wage worker in Mexico, China, or Cambodia." The review thinks that Bremmer's style, "so fast, fluent, and sure-footed on TV— is less effective in book form." The reviewer prefers to see Bremmer working out more "of the contradictions in his arguments and pursue his thoughts in more depth." There are contradictions about his views on

China's economy, jobs, and aging population, for example. Bremmer accordingly concludes with "some particularly ill-timed faith in technocratic solutions, praising Facebook for building communities and lauding its chairman Mark Zuckerberg." The review also appreciates Bremmer for "connecting the dots between developments that may seem distant and unrelated." There is, however, the risk of "hewing so close to the news."

Us vs.Them a *New York Times* bestseller by the author of *Every Nation for Itself* and *The J Curve.*

Discussion Questions

"Get Ready to Enter a New World"

Tip: Begin with questions dealing with broader issues to ensure ample time for quality discussions. Read through all discussion questions before engaging.

question 1

The author shows how globalization has destabilized the United States, Europe, and the developing world particularly countries like Mexico, Turkey, and Brazil. How has have developing countries like Mexico, Turkey, and Brazil been destabilized by globalization?

~ ~ ~

~~~

question 2

Bremmer believes globalization has done good things. It has enabled economic growth and helped many populations out of poverty. Can you cite countries where globalization has helped the poor? How has globalization alleviated poverty in these countries?

~~~

~~~

question 3

The world is seeing the rise of nationalist and populist politicians who lead their countries in attacking the media, other political leaders, and the corporate elite in their efforts to blame "them" for the economic uncertainty that populations are going through. Can you cite examples of these charismatic politicians? In which countries do they rule? Why do their people elect them? What do these politicians promise their people?

~~~

~ ~ ~

question 4

The gap between the elite and the poor has widened over the years. "Forty-two people in the world have the same wealth as the bottom 50 percent," he writes. How do you feel about this inequality?

~ ~ ~

~~~

question 5

He explains that "when infrastructure spending, public school systems, health care and the like are tied directly to the economic fortunes of a community, it compounds problems of inequality." How does this show in your own community? What services suffer because of lack of government budget?

~~~

~~~

question 6

Workers are threatened by other people flowing across borders because they see this as threats to their livelihoods, lives, entitlements, and status. "Donald Trump understood this better than any of his political rivals in the U.S." and his supporters continue to believe him "because no one else in the United States can credibly promise to defend their interests against establishment disdain." Do you agree with this analysis? Why? Why not?

~~~

question 7

In the book's introduction, Bremmer shares his family's working-class origins, his rise to professional and academic success, and the fulfillment of his American dream. He asks himself why the American dream cannot work for everybody else. Why does he include personal details in the book?

question 8

In Chapter One, he starts with a quote from William Ernest Henley: "I am the master of my fate, I am the captain of my soul." Why does the author place this at the start of the chapter? What is its significance to the chapter's content?

~~~

question 9

The book closes with a chapter on the relevance of a social contract that binds governments and their citizens. What does he say about the importance of a social contract? Do you think this is a practical solution to the problems posed by globalization?

~~~

~ ~ ~

question 10

Bremmer says that the mentality of "us vs. them" will intensify "before governments change their ways." Do you agree? Why? Why not?

~ ~ ~

~~~

question 11

The book cites the author's analysis of developments in countries like Nigeria, Venezuela, Saudi Arabia, India, China, and Russia and shows the common factors that incite the "us vs. them" mentality. What are these common factors? Do you recognize them happening in your country?

~~~

~~~

question 12

He predicts that these countries "will erect physical and technological 'walls' to keep people in line, and Europe and the United States will follow suit, becoming more protectionist as the developing world struggles." Do you think the trend of protectionism can be reversed? What can be done to prevent it?

~~~

~~~

question 13

He says: "It's one thing for the government to transfer large amounts of wealth to people who need it…it's another to provide them with the services that middle-class citizens expect." He thinks some countries will struggle with providing services for its citizens, particularly those with rapidly aging populations like Japan, Germany, and the Nordic countries. What are other social services beginning to decline in your community? How has globalization impacted on these services?

~~~

~~~

question 14

Bremmer shares his analysis of the global use of robotics and artificial intelligence technology. This will accordingly reduce "the low-wage advantage that helps poor countries...A shoe manufacturer in Kentucky is better off replacing a middle-wage worker with a no-wage robot than with a low-wage worker in Mexico, China, or Cambodia." How do you feel about robots taking over your job? Can you prevent your job from being taken over by robotics?

~~~

question 15

The book cites that political conflict is not anymore about the divide between the left and the right or between the West and the non-West. It is between the rich and those whose economic status is unstable and seek protection from threatening economic competition, foreigners, and technological change. What is the conflict between the left and right all about? Don't you think Bremmer's ideas are more leftist?

~~~

~ ~ ~

question 16

Kirkus Reviews says the book is a clear and logical analysis of the phenomena of Trump and Brexit. A "lucid and provocative" book, it gives a warning of what could happen in the future. What scenario can you see happening in the future that this book hints about? How would you see yourself or your family adjusting to this future?

~ ~ ~

~~~

question 17

Publishers Weekly review thinks Bremmer gives "an astute but not optimistic analysis" which could be "difficult reading for those overwhelmed by the current political climate." Did you have a difficult time reading this book? What part do you find particularly hard to read? Why?

~~~

~~~

question 18

The Wall Street Journal review thinks that Bremmer's style, "so fast, fluent, and sure-footed on TV— is less effective in book form." The reviewer prefers to see Bremmer working out more "of the contradictions in his arguments and pursue his thoughts in more depth." There are contradictions about his views on China's economy, jobs, and an aging population, for example. Have you noted any contradictions in the book? Can you share them?

~~~

~ ~ ~

question 19

WSJ further says that Bremmer concludes with "some particularly ill-timed faith in technocratic solutions, praising Facebook for building communities and lauding its chairman Mark Zuckerberg." Do you agree with Bremmer on his view of Zuckerberg? Why? Why not?

~ ~ ~

~ ~ ~

question 20

Bremmer is cited for "connecting the dots between developments that may seem distant and unrelated." What connected dots particularly enlightened you? How are you enlightened by these connected dots?

~ ~ ~

Introducing the Author

Ian Arthur Bremmer is a political scientist who has authored a book on U.S. foreign policy, global political risk, and states in transition. His books include *Every Nation for Itself, The J Curve,* and the bestselling *Us vs. Them: The Failure of Globalism.* He founded Eurasia Group, a research organization which focuses on political risk. The group has offices in New York City, Tokyo, Singapore, Sao Paulo, London, and San Francisco. He teaches at New York University.

Bremmer and his brother were raised by his mother in Chelsea, Massachusetts. His father was a soldier in the Korean War. He died when Bremmer was four, and his mother single-handedly raised him and his sibling. They lived in a housing project area. A program called "Teach a Kid How America Works" gave him the chance to visit Boston's high-rise buildings and meet the men who worked within. One of the men told him and the other children who visited that they too can work in those buildings and nobody can stop them if they wanted to. The man said they could be successful if the study hard and work hard. Bremmer finished college with a scholarship and then earned a Ph.D., launched his own company, appeared on TV, and wrote books. As a young adult, he believed that globalism and capitalism gave everybody a chance to be successful in life. He said he devoted his professional life working within the system work but realized that it doesn't work for everybody. He cites the rioting that happened in 1999 at a meeting for World Trade Organization members. It was a warning sign, he said, but the globalists didn't pay attention.

He finished his bachelors in International Relations from Tulane University and his Ph.D. in Political Science from Stanford University. He first taught at the Hoover Institution and in 1998 launched Eurasia Group. He also taught at Columbia University, the World Policy Institute, the EastWest Institute, and at Lawrence Livermore National Laboratory. He was awarded the Harold J. Newman Distinguished Fellow in Geopolitics by the Asia

Society Policy Institute. His national bestselling book *Every Nation For Itself: Winners and Losers in a G-Zero World* (2012) explains the importance of global leadership in the world order, identifying the opportunities and risks that come with it. His book *The End of the Free Market: Who Wins the War Between States and Corporations* (2010) describes state capitalism as implemented by countries all over the world and identifies its economic and political effects. His book *The J Curve: A New Way to Understand Why Nations Rise and Fall* was published in 2006 and cited as one of the best books of the year by *The Economist*. In his article for Time magazine, Bremmer says the internet and social media has caused political fragmentation which manifests in the real world through election results. He warns that automation and artificial intelligence will cost "400 to 800 million people their jobs by 2030." The economic gains resulting from using robots at the workplace will go to people who have control of the technology. He thinks the world should prepare for "a 'post-industrial revolution,'...that is set to widen the chasm between 'us' and 'them' still further." He cautions that the polarized situation that the world is experiencing now could lead to the destruction of the interconnected world with just "one global economic stumble."

Bonus Downloads

*Get Free Books with **<u>Any Purchase</u>** of Conversation Starters!*

Every purchase comes with a FREE download!

Add spice to any conversation
Never run out of things to say
Spend time with those you love

Get it Now

<u>or Click Here.</u>

Scan Your Phone

Fireside Questions

"What would you do?"

Tip: These questions can be a fun exercise as it spurs creativity among the readers by allowing alternate scene endings and "if this was you" questions.

~~~

question 21

Bremmer and his brother were raised by his mother in Chelsea, Massachusetts. His father was a soldier in the Korean War. He died when Bremmer was four, and his mother single-handedly raised him and his sibling. They lived in a housing project area. A program called "Teach a Kid How America Works" gave him the chance to visit Boston's high-rise buildings and meet the men who worked within. What was his experience in meeting the people inside the buildings? How did this change his life?

~~~

~~~

question 22

Bremmer finished college with a scholarship and then earned a Ph.D., launched his own company, appeared on TV, and wrote books. As a young adult, he believed that globalism and capitalism gave everybody a chance to be successful in life. He said he devoted his professional life working within the system work but realized that it doesn't work for everybody. How does he feel about globalization now?

~~~

question 23

His national bestselling book Every Nation For Itself: Winners and Losers in a G-Zero World (2012) explains the importance of global leadership in the world order, identifying the opportunities and risks that come with it. His book The End of the Free Market: Who Wins the War Between States and Corporations (2010) describes state capitalism as implemented by countries all over the world and identifies its economic and political effects. His book The J Curve: A New Way to Understand Why Nations Rise and Fall was published in 2006 and cited as one of the best books of the year by The Economist. Have you read any of these books? What is common in all these books?

~~~

~~~

question 24

He warns that automation and artificial intelligence will cost "400 to 800 million people their jobs by 2030." The economic gains resulting from using robots at the workplace will go to people who have control of the technology. He thinks the world should prepare for "a 'post-industrial revolution,'…that is set to widen the chasm between 'us' and 'them' still further." What comes to mind when you think of post-industrial revolution? How will this widen the chasm between us and them?

~~~

~ ~ ~

question 25

He cautions that the polarized situation that the
world is experiencing now could lead to the
destruction of the interconnected world with just
"one global economic stumble." What images come
to mind when you think about the destruction of
the interconnected world?

~ ~ ~

~~~

question 26

The gap between the elite and the poor has widened over the years. "Forty-two people in the world have the same wealth as the bottom 50 percent," he writes. If you are one of the 42 people, how would you feel about those in the bottom 50 percent? What would you do?

~~~

question 27

Kirkus Reviews says the book is a clear and logical analysis of the phenomena of Trump and Brexit. A "lucid and provocative" book, it gives a warning of what could happen in the future. If Trump's supporters read this book, do you think they will change his view about him? Why? Why not?

question 28

Critics say Bremmer accordingly concludes with "some particularly ill-timed faith in technocratic solutions, praising Facebook for building communities and lauding its chairman Mark Zuckerberg." If you are Bremmer, what would you say about Zuckerberg? What would you suggest for him to do to help make globalization work for the poor?

~ ~ ~

~~~

question 29

A review by the Wall Street Journal says Bremmer's view is dark and pessimistic that he "even frets about places where recent social and economic progress has been great — China, India, and Turkey…even Russia." If you are to suggest to Bremmer to lighten the tone of his book, what would you say?

~~~

~ ~ ~

question 30

Recent developments show that nations are becoming more closed and people becoming tribal. The grand project of creating an international order does not anymore appear to be possible. If nations do become closed and tribal, how would you envision how the world will be like? Is there a positive result from this?

~ ~ ~

Quiz Questions

"Ready to Announce the Winners?"

Tip: Create a leaderboard and track scores to see who gets the most correct answers. Winners required. Prizes optional.

~~~

quiz question 1

The gap between the elite and the poor has widened over the years. _____ people in the world have the same wealth as the bottom 50 percent.

~~~

~~~

quiz question 2

Workers are threatened by other people flowing across borders because they see this as threats to their livelihoods, lives, entitlements, and status. _____ understood this better than any of his political rivals in the U.S. and his supporters continue to believe him because no one else in the United States can credibly promise to defend their interests against establishment disdain.

~~~

~~~

quiz question 3

In the book's _____, Bremmer shares his family's working-class origins, his rise to professional and academic success, and the fulfillment of his American dream. He asks himself why the American dream cannot work for everybody else.

~~~

quiz question 4

True or False: The author gives five factors that are behind the divisions between "us" and "them." The first is Economics, which shows that the gap between the elite and the poor has widened over the years.

~~~

quiz question 5

True or False: In Chapter One, he starts with a
quote from William Blake: "I am the master of my
fate, I am the captain of my soul."

~~~

~~~

quiz question 6

True or False: The book cites that political conflict is not anymore about the divide between the left and the right or between the West and the non-West. It is between the rich and those whose economic status is unstable and seek protection from threatening economic competition, foreigners, and technological change.

~~~

~~~

quiz question 7

True or False: The author shows how globalization has destabilized the United States, Europe, and the developing world particularly countries like Mexico, Turkey, and Brazil. He says nations have to make stark choices; they could start building walls or they could create new arrangements that bind citizens and governments together that allow both parties to better deal with a world of increasing interdependence.

~~~

~~~

quiz question 8

He founded _____ a research organization which focuses on political risk. The group has offices in New York City, Tokyo, Singapore, Sao Paulo, London, and San Francisco.

~~~

~~~

quiz question 9

His book _____ (2010) describes state capitalism as implemented by countries all over the world and identifies its economic and political effects.

~~~

~~~

quiz question 10

True or False: In his article for Time magazine, Bremmer says the internet and social media has caused political fragmentation which manifests in the real world through election results.

~~~

~ ~ ~

quiz question 11

True or False: He finished his bachelors in International Relations from Tulane University and his Ph.D. in Political Science from Harvard University.

~ ~ ~

~ ~ ~

quiz question 12

True or False: As a young adult, he believed that globalism and capitalism gave everybody a chance to be successful in life. He said he devoted his professional life working within the system work but realized that it doesn't work for everybody.

~ ~ ~

Quiz Answers

1. Forty-two
2. Donald Trump
3. Introduction
4. True
5. False
6. True
7. True
8. Eurasia Group
9. The End of the Free Market: Who Wins the War Between States and Corporations
10. True
11. False
12. True

Ways to Continue Your Reading

E VERY month, our team runs through a wide selection of books to pick the best titles for readers and reading groups, and promotes these titles to our thousands of readers – sometimes with free downloads, sale dates, and additional brochures.

Click here to sign up for these benefits.

If you have not yet read the original work or would like to read it again, you can purchase the original book here.

Bonus Downloads

*Get Free Books with **<u>Any Purchase</u>** of Conversation Starters!*

Every purchase comes with a FREE download!

Add spice to any conversation
Never run out of things to say
Spend time with those you love

Get it Now

<u>or Click Here.</u>

Scan Your Phone

On the Next Page...

If you found this book helpful to your discussions and rate it a 4 or 5, please write us a review on the next page.

Any length would be fine but we'd appreciate hearing you more! We'd be very encouraged.

Till next time,

BookHabits

"Loving Books is Actually a Habit"

CPSIA information can be obtained
at www.ICGtesting.com
Printed in the USA
BVHW070745110620
581224BV00003B/169

9 780368 075926